GIANNIS ANTEOKOUNMPO

THE STORY OF HOW GIANNIS ANTEOKOUNMPO BECAME THE MOST DOMINANT PLAYER IN THE NBA

By

JACKSON CARTER

Copyright © 2020

TABLE OF CONTENTS

LEGAL NOTES

CHILDHOOD

The game of basketball has evolved. No longer are we seeing the same types of players in the NBA that we used to see even fifteen years ago. Instead, new players are coming into the league that never could have played in the same game if the players of old were still there. Similarly, fans are getting to experience a new game as well, seeing a new breed of player that many are falling in love with.

Many are often asked about who their favorite player is. In today's society, many fans, both young and old, have a lot of names to choose from. There are retired players like Michael Jordan or Magic Johnson, then there are the more contemporary names like Steph Curry and LeBron James. Whether fans are looking at overall performance, loyal to a specific team, or are just fans of the game in general, nobody can deny that those names worked hard to earn their place in the conversation.

However, more people, especially young immigrants in Greece, are calling out another name into the discussion: Giannis Antetokounmpo, who is also known as the "Greek Freak." The young star has been turning a lot of heads for the past few years in the league, and in interviews comes off as a pleasant, cheery young man. However, few have looked back at his life and seen the trials that he has gone through to really appreciate that uplifting outlook that he offers to the world.

Giannis was born in Athens, Greece, on December 6, 1994, to Charles and Veronica Antetokounmpo. The couple had moved to Greece just a few years earlier, emigrating from their home in Lagos, Nigeria. There, they had already had a son, Francis, but had lived a life of little opportunity. They decided to move to Greece in the hopes that the move would open their lives up to better job prospects and the ability to provide a better experience for their growing family. They ended up staying in Greece, having Giannis and then three other sons, Thanasis, Kostas, and Alex, all of whom were given Greek names in honor of their new home. Francis, too, would join the family in Greece later on, leaving the grandparents who had raised him in Nigeria.

However, despite the hope that Greece would provide a better life for the Antetokounmpo family, things were tough for them instead. The family, despite the boys being born in Greece, were not granted citizenship, making the boys neither citizens of Nigeria nor their home in Greece. This forced the family to be ostracized by in the highly charged Greece of the 1990s. This was a time of economic hardship and many were struggling at the time. Immigrants like the Antetokounmpo family were often blamed or took the brunt of the anger and frustration that swelled in the country.

That being so, both Charles and Veronic had difficulty providing for their young family. They were isolated, denied national health care, access to sports leagues for the boys, and many of the better-paying jobs like those in civil service. Instead, Charles and Veronica worked odd jobs when they could be found, doing everything from picking oranges to working as a handyman or a babysitter. Even so, putting food on the table and affording the bills was a constant concern for the family. They lived in fear of being sent back to Nigeria. Since the boys had been born in

Greece, that future in Nigeria was just as uncertain as the one that they had in Greece.

Living in the low socioeconomic neighborhood of Sepola, Greece, the family moved around a lot. When they weren't able to afford the rent on their two-bedroom apartment (Giannis and his three brothers all sharing the same room), they were forced to move. They spent these years continually looking for the place that would have the lowest rent in the hopes that they'd be able to afford it. As the boys grew up, they, too, helped the family make ends meat.

Going out on the street, scrawny and hungry, Giannis and his brothers could be found peddling things like sunglasses or purses on street corners. They would sell all day in the hope that they could make some money to take home that evening. His younger brother, Thanasis, recalls that even making $10 in a day was enough because it meant that they wouldn't go to bed starving that night. Many today would imagine this situation and wonder how a young man who went through this could be the same smiling, optimistic man they see on their televisions. But, Giannis only looks back on it as a time when the family struggled, yes, but something that they accepted as a part of their life. He even makes a joke when asked about it now, saying that he was a cute kid, so that helped them sell more on the streets.

Additionally, with the climate in Greece at the time, families like Gainnis's stuck out and were often the target of hate crimes and violence. However, Giannis and his brothers recall that they don't remember being targeted themselves, and instead share about the times when they were treated with hospitality and kindness. For example, a neighbor gave the boys clothes that they no longer fit. In fact, a local café would offer the boys breakfast each morning, despite the locals looking down on the act for encouraging the outsiders. Despite the tough situations that they were forced into, the boys recall growing up in a home that was filled with love. Even when they lacked the money or the food or resources that they worked for there was no shortage of love in the household.

One way that the growing boys dealt with the hardships was to turn to sports. Charles was a former professional soccer player and Veronica a former high jumper, it seemed only natural that their sons would also be athletically inclined. With the background of soccer, many like the Antetokounmpo boys were drawn to soccer. However, the boys participated in many sports, taking home several medals at the local church events regardless of what sport it was for. This helped many see the boys, and their family, as more than just immigrants, their athletic ability allowed people to see them as more than outsiders.

Eventually, at the age of seven, Giannis and his brother Thanasis turned toward basketball, playing pick up games in one of the local park's courts. They weren't very good, but they loved the escape that being on the court offered them. Having very little, though, even presented them with challenges here. When they first began playing, the two boys would have to take turns, unlacing and exchanging the one pair of sneakers that they had for the other brother to get his court time.

As the boys grew, their natural talents allowed them to have fun, but they weren't ever really trained to play. In fact, one friend who met Giannis when they were both eleven, would recall that Giannis wasn't very good growing up. Although he loved to play, Giannis was just a skinny, bumbling kid on the court, struggling even to dribble or shoot properly. Still, though, it was something that they both enjoyed, and it helped to keep him positive as his family went through their struggles.

DISCOVERY IN THE PARK

It was on one of those days at the park that Giannis's life was forever changed. Spiros Velliniatis, who had played as a foreign exchange student in Florida, was a Greek coach for the junior squad of an amateur team, and he was looking for players. However, his own recruitment process wasn't what you would typically think of. Instead of looking for athletes at the tournaments, schools, or games, Velliniatis was different. He was looking for the diamond in the rough. In fact, he said that during that time, around the time when Giannis was 13 years old, he would often travel the neighborhoods that were known to have a high immigrant population. He would look for young athletic boys, had a frame that looked like it would grow to a basketball type physique, and, most importantly, he paid attention to their spirits.

When Velliniatis saw Giannis chasing his brothers around the playground one afternoon, something caught his eye in the way that Giannis moved and played. He could see that Giannis could change direction quickly in the game of tag, probably thanks to his father's love of soccer and the footwork that he bestowed on his boys. Additionally, Velliniatis saw the awareness and energy that Giannis had, which was precisely what Velliniatis was looking for. He knew that, with Giannis's frame and his natural abilities, he would have the frame to be a great basketball player. If he was able to pair this with the spatial awareness, Giannis could be coached to be great at any sport that he set his heart to.

So, Velliniatis approached the boys and asked them to summon Veronica, who was busy cleaning houses nearby. When she approached, Velliniatis told her how he would like Giannis to play for his team. He even promised the family 800 euro a month if Giannis would play. This would help to ease the burden of finances that would be created if Giannis wasn't out there working to sell things on the streets. Velliniatis knew that many of the Nigerian based families were only interested in soccer. If he was going to get the Antetokounmpo family to agree to let Giannis play, he needed to convince them of what it could be worth.

Needless to say, his plan was effective. Giannis began to play for Filathlitikos, but his new teammates were less than impressed. In fact, the team captain recalls seeing Giannis the first time and wondering what on earth the coach had been thinking in recruiting him. Giannis could barely dribble and struggled with a basic layup, forcing many to look at Giannis and immediately begin to doubt his place on the team. However, soon after starting to practice with the team, his teammates and those around them began to take note of something special, just like their coach had seen.

Velliniatis coached the team on fundamentals. He drilled them hard until they all got them just right, even Giannis, who was seemingly behind the curve. Giannis's ability to grasp the game and his work ethic made a huge impact on his team. Despite being years behind his teammates, Giannis was extremely competitive and hated to lose. Giannis would push himself harder and farther than his teammates to be able to compete with them.

Velliniatis pushed everyone on the team to learn ball handling and passing, enabling them all to be flexible on the court. With this help, Giannis found himself being able to play at any position that was needed of him. Giannis learned how to use his natural footwork and agility to help him make an impact as he worked on the rest of his skills. Giannis was so dedicated, in fact, that he would often stay and workout in the gym past midnight, sleeping on a mat in the weight room instead of returning home. During that time, racist and violent gangs and groups were known to pick on immigrant families. Giannis was able to dedicate himself to basketball while still keeping himself safe after dark instead of risking the long walk home.

After continuing to work on his skills, he was quickly becoming the player that Velliniatis had hoped that he would become when he saw him playing tag on that playground. In 2011, Giannis moved up to the men's team, at 17 years old, playing as part of the Greek 3rd Division, the third level semi-pro league. Here, Giannis and his brother Thanasis continued to work hard and increase their skills. They were able to turn the game that they'd played to escape a harsh reality into something that they were passionate about and loved.

Rise to Prominance

Then, in 2012, Giannis was pulled up to the Greek A2 League, bumping up to the 2nd tier semi-pro team for the Filathlitikos. He was no longer the stumbling, bumbling boy that had begun playing, now he was making a massive impact on his team and on the Greek league in general. He and his brother helped bring their team to the forefront of their league. Their impact forced many in Europe to turn their heads and notice him as a young up and coming prospect.

That season, Giannis played in 26 games, averaging 22.5 minutes per game. During this time, he racked in 9.5 points, 5.2 rebounds, 1.4 assists, and 1.0 blocks on average per game. He was even selected by coaches in the league to play in the Greek League All-Star Game as a special player. He hadn't actually been voted an All-Star, but the coaches wanted him to play in the game just the same. It seemed that they had taken a look at the up and coming player and saw the potential that he had, and perhaps they hoped to see how he would fare against the All-Stars as well.

This great season, and his ability to turn heads with his skills, his agility, and his positive outlook, drew many European clubs to seek after Giannis. Just two days after he turned 18 that year, Giannis even signed with CAI Zaragoza, a Spanish team, for a four-year contract that offered NBA buyout options after each season. This would mean starting his life as an adult by moving to a new country, playing professional basketball, and possibly making enough money to help his family out.

However, his plans to move to Spain in order to play were for naught. By the end of the season, NBA teams were already lining up to take a look at Giannis.

As his career was beginning to get bigger and bigger, it was made even more difficult by his inability to travel. Due to the rocky climate in Greece, all paperwork, including giving passports to immigrants or children of immigrants like Giannis, was put on hold for two years. Even though he and his brothers had been born in the country, because their parents came their illegally and had no papers, the boys were not seen as Greek citizens. They, therefore, were not allowed to be granted any documents themselves. This meant that Giannis never had the opportunity to play in the big tournaments outside of Greece.

That made it difficult for Giannis to get his name out even further. He hoped to have the issue resolved before he planned on making a move to Spain to fulfill his contract with CAI Zaragoza. However, due to his rise in the basketball sphere, the Internal Minister himself worked his magic through the system and personally took care of Giannis's and Thanasis's paperwork, ensuring that they were now considered Greek citizens in May of 2013, which allowed them to travel with their newly printed passports.

This allowed Giannis the ability to play in a European tournament, the FIBA Under-20 Championship. At this tournament, all thirty NBA teams sent coaches or scouts to look at the talent overseas. Giannis had a fantastic set of games, leading his team to an 8–2 record and carving out the second spot in defensive rebounds and the seventh spot for blocked shots during the tournament. He averaged only eight points but had 7.6 rebounds and 2.2 assists per game. It was there that many of the NBA coaches began to get really interested in Giannis, and they were finally able to see him play in person. Coaches said that when they saw him play as the point guard for his team, he made good choices and handled the ball well. This made him a solid potential prospect for the NBA at multiple positions.

NBA Draft

After this dominant performance Giannis was ready to take the NBA. The NBA Draft was set to take place on June 27th. Now that the teams had been able to see Giannis play in person, he was expected to go in the first round. He and his brother, Thanasis, headed to the draft with their agents, ready to see if the NBA was going to take a chance on a young, 18-year-old boy from Greece. This was a massive moment for Giannis. Not only was he heading to the United States, but he was approaching the moment that he'd worked so hard for. He would finally have the chance to enter the NBA and becoming a professional basketball player in the US.

His agent, Alex Saratsis asked Giannis what color the suit was that Giannis was going to wear to the draft as they boarded the plane for the US. Giannis looked at him in disbelief, asking where he would have possibly been able to get a suit from. Luckily, they were able to get him a suit, and he wore it stylishly, as he and his brother sat down at the draft and listened to the first round picks beginning to be called out.

Without really getting to see much of him before the draft, teams were hesitant to draft Giannis due to his young age and relative inexperience in the higher levels of competition. His body was compared to that of Kevin Durant's, but he was still skinny and seemingly lean compared to the players he'd be going up against. Although he'd done well in the semi-pro league, many knew that he needed a lot of development and was more of a long-term pick than others that were in his draft class. Still, Giannis was hopeful that his talent, his determination, and his attitude would be enough for a team to take a chance on him.

As the first round commenced, Canadian Anthony Bennett was selected by the Cleveland Cavaliers. He was followed by Victor Oladipo, Otto Porter, and Cody Zeller. But, with the fifteenth pick overall, the Milwaukee Bucks selected Giannis. When his name was called, he smiled, rose up as his brother hoisted the Greek flag. Giannis exchanged some hugs with his brother and agent before making his way down to the stage and getting to put on his Milwaukee Bucks cap. He had made it into the NBA.

In the post-draft interviews, Giannis was shocked, excited to think that this moment had finally come. He was still in awe of the whole process and found it hard to speak about what it felt like at the moment. Still, he was able to share that he was feeling like his dream had finally come true. He shared that he had come from a childhood and life of struggle, where his family worked hard to have a better life. He knew now that he had been drafted, he and his family would finally have that better life. He commented about how his parents would be proud of him. He knew that their hard work and effort over the years had led up to this moment. Now he would be able to ensure that they didn't have to work like that anymore.

Being selected fifteenth overall led Giannis to become Greece's highest selected player in the NBA draft. He was also the youngest player in the draft that year. Although many knew he would need years to develop to be fully NBA worthy, they had high hopes that Giannis would have a bright future ahead of him. His brother, Thanasis was drafted to the Delaware 87ers in the NBA developmental league. Thanasis moved with him to the US where they both began to live a new life different from anything that they could have ever imagined back on those courts, sharing the same set of sneakers just to be able to play for a few minutes.

After all those years of working on the streets to make a few dollars to help their family, both Giannis and Thanasis were hopeful that this wouldn't just end with an NBA contract, but it could also mean something new and amazing for their family. While both boys were proud of where they came from and knew that they had lived a life of struggle and had found moments of joy within it, there was also the hope that those struggles were now a thing of the past. As they moved to the US, they were excited to start a new adventure and to be able to really help alleviate the stress of money from their parents' lives.

A PROMISING START

In his rookie season, Giannis worked hard to show that he deserved to be out there on the court, playing the game he'd worked so hard to get good at. The lanky, young man who had left Greece was doing all that he could to up his game and make the Bucks, Greece, and his family proud.

Still, he had his doubters. When looking at his build compared to the other players in the NBA, Giannis still looked like a young boy, his arms and legs as thin as rails, and paired with his height, he looked like a young man who hadn't yet grown into his own body. Similarly, many people were wondering how you took someone from a semi-pro team overseas and thrust him into the most competitive league on the planet. Some believed that he should be developed in the developmental league first. Still, the Bucks decided to invest their time and effort in keeping Giannis at the pro level and letting him see what he was up against. Luckily, that natural competitive spirit that Giannis had always had led him to up his game in a short matter of time.

He played in 77 games that season, averaging 6.8 points and 4.4 rebounds. He had twenty-three games where he scored over ten points in a game and two games where he had more than ten rebounds. He had two double-doubles that season as well. Giannis also finished the season with 61 blocks, more than any other rookie that year. Although he was making an excellent start to his NBA career, the team wasn't doing very well and didn't make it to the playoffs that season. Still, Giannis was gaining traction in the NBA and was invited to the Rising Stars Challenge during the NBA All-Star Weekend as well as being selected NBA All-Rookie Second Team.

During the Rising Stars Challenge, Giannis made a good showing, but only put up nine points in his seventeen minutes of play. Many of the other young players were dead set on putting up jump shots each time they got the ball, but Giannis wasn't playing that same style. Instead, he managed to sink his three field goals and three from four at the free-throw line. Also, he created a buzzer-beating highlight style dunk on an unguarded fast break as the second quarter drew to a close.

In watching him play that rookie season, it was clear that the Bucks had made a good pick. Not only did they gain some height and ball control, they were able to get a young prospect that would help them in rebuilding the franchise. It seemed like their bet that his natural abilities and his determination to win would pay off in the coming years was going to pay off. Giannis never played like he was anything less than an NBA player. Despite those who doubted him, his rookie season showed the world that he wasn't afraid to go toe to toe with the bigs in the paint or to defend or play against veterans beyond the arc. His quick feet and excellent court vision made him a great addition to the team. On top of that, upon entering the league, Giannis was about 6' 8.5" tall. By the time his rookie season was over, he had grown two and a half inches to a whopping 6' 11". This provided him with the length to traverse the court quickly and easily as well as towering over many of those who guarded him.

During that first season, it is rumored that Giannis did everything he could to send as much of his paycheck home to his family in Greece as he could. In fact, he would even deny himself the ability to take a cab to practices. Instead, he chooses to jog because he claimed that his family could use the money he would have spent sitting in the cab much better than he could have.

The following season, from 2014-2015, Giannis continued to develop. He was now getting more comfortable with the league, and a year's worth of professional, experienced training helped Giannis begin to fill out his skills and his body. This year, he only missed a single game and had several great showings. One of those was when they Bucks faced the Houston Rockets, and Giannis scored 27 points and pulled down 15 rebounds. This game's performance earned him the Eastern Conference Player of the Week. He was again invited back to the All-Star Weekend, this time to compete in the dunk contest, and if you had watched his regular-season games, you'd know why.

Play after play on his sophomore highlight reel feature Giannis driving to the hole to slam it home. Not only does he do this on steals and fast breaks, but he even does it when facing man to man coverage. He can defeat some of the NBA's veteran players who just can't seem to guard his quick-footed moves where each stride takes him five feet closer to the rim. Whether it is on a fast break or under heavy pressure in the paint, there are tons of dunks and layups that feature Giannis showing the world that he can move that long body of his in a ton of creative ways.

However, unable to sink his first dunk in the given attempts, he got marked down considerably, scoring just sixes across the board. For his second dunk, however, he brought out his younger brother Thanasis, for the assist. Both of the brothers heading toward the hoop from opposite sidelines, Thanasis lofts it up to his older brother, who grabbed it, passes in front of the hoop, and then slams it in behind his head before coming back down. Although he completed the dunk this time, even scoring a selfie with his brother afterward, the judges gave him a mix of sevens and a six and eight, not giving him enough points to advance to the next round.

That season, the Bucks had a better run as well. Not only did they finish 6th in the East, but they also made it to the playoffs, giving Giannis his first taste of the postseason. Although they fell to the Chicago Bulls in six games, Giannis had shown that he was, despite his initial doubters, still able to play with the big boys. Throughout the season, Giannis averaged 12.7 points and 6.7 rebounds per game. This led the Bucks to extend his rookie contract for the following season.

BUILDING SKILLS AND ATTENTION

At the beginning of the season, on August first, the NBA paired up with FIBA and the first-ever NBA exhibition game took place at Ellis Park Arena in Johannesburg, South Africa. It was the first game featuring Team Africa vs. Team World and was part of the Basketball Without Borders initiative. Team Africa was made up of NBA players who had either had a parent born in Africa or who had been born in Africa. Team World was mainly players from the NBA, but also featured a few international players as well.

During this game, Giannis played for Team Africa, representing the continent where his father and mother had been born and where they had lived before emigrating to Greece. As the only player on Team Africa capable of handling the ball well enough to play point guard, Giannis got the opportunity to play in a position that he didn't typically play. However, he did extremely well in the game, going up against Chris Paul for Team World.

The game featured a lot of great plays and teams comprised of players who had never played together well. Players like Luol Deng and Luc Mbah A Moute played alongside Giannis. They were just as thrilled as he was to be able to represent Team Africa. For all of the players, there was an excited and proud atmosphere about the whole game. They were thrilled that they got to represent the continent in the very first NBA exhibition game to take place there. The commissioner and others like Hakeem Olajuwon were also in attendance, Olajuwon who had made huge strides as an African player in the NBA, was also excited to be a part of the game.

Still, the sold-out crowd was excited to see a number of great plays and bouts of teamwork, especially in the second half, when things became more competitive. Giannis dominated on the fast breaks for Team Africa. He did a fantastic job of setting his teammates up, putting his excellent court vision to use to help Team Africa stay close. Additionally, Giannis was able to keep up his usual repertoire of driving to the hole moves and made it look easy. It was almost like he wasn't being guarded by some of the NBA's top players. This was an excellent opportunity for Giannis to represent part of his heritage and to get to travel to the continent of his parent's birth for the first time.

As the 2015-2016 season commenced, Giannis continued to make his mark on the court. Starting to fill out with bigger arms and legs, he still went on to dominate the approach style game as he would often create plays by driving to the hole, either finishing it himself or passing it off slyly to one of his teammates. In one game against the Brooklyn Nets, Giannis, even under pressure, picks up his dribble just past the three-point line, fakes the pass, and then takes it in for the dunk. His ability to cover so much room in only two steps makes him a threat like no other guard out there. He was even compared to being a 6'11" version of Russel Westbrook as he creates openings for his teammates and can find them even when double-teamed.

That season, he averaged 16 points per game in just the first 20 games. He even managed to bring in 33 points in the Milwaukee defeat to the Cleveland Cavaliers. Along with his teammates, the Bucks stopped the undefeated streak of the Golden State Warriors with Giannis contributing 11 points, 12 rebounds, and 8 assists in the win. Later that season, Giannis had his first-ever triple-double against the Los Angeles Lakers. He scored 27 points, had 12 rebounds, and 10 assists. At just 21 years of age, this triple-double made Giannis the youngest ever Bucks player to have a triple-double. But he wasn't done there. No, by the end of the season, he had a fantastic five triple-doubles to his name. The Bucks missed the playoffs that season, but that didn't stop them from extending Giannis's contract for another season.

The next year, Giannis had finally come into his own. He no longer looked like the young kid who had come into the league and America as a skinny young player. He now had filled out, and it was clear that he had been spending time in the gym as well as doing weight training and drills in the offseason. When comparing his photo from just a few years before, he was almost unrecognizable. Many, as well as Giannis, attributed much of his growth to working so closely with former NBA star Jason Kidd. Kidd spent many hours helping Giannis to develop in the player that he was becoming.

All of his hard work was finally coming to fruition and his numbers were starting to show it. In the season opener against the Charlotte Hornets, Giannis scored 31 points, kicking the season off with a bang despite the team's loss. During December, he was named the Eastern Conference Player of the Week for his matchup against the Brooklyn Nets. And that was just the beginning. Giannis would go on to have his best season yet, setting a strong tone for himself and launching himself into the record books.

With over 20 points in 14 consecutive games, Giannis matched former Bucks player, Michale Redd, for the longest streak since 2006. Additionally, he was selected as a starter of the 2017 All-Star Game. This, again, helped etch Giannis's name solidly in the Bucks franchise record book since he was the first All-Star player since Redd in 2006, the first All-Star starter since Sidney Moncrief back in 1986. He was also the youngest player, at just twenty-two years of age, in Bucks history to start an All-Star Game and the first Greek player to become an NBA All-Star. Not only did he make it to the team, but he performed exceedingly well, leading the East team with 30 points that game.

Joining Redd, Moncrief, and Terry Cummings, as the only other Bucks players, Giannis was later named the Conference Player of the Month for March. He led the Bucks in all five major stat categories as well: points, rebounds, assists, steals, and blocks. He was clearly an impact player and a force to be reckoned with on the court. In fact, there are only four other players before Giannis, from any team, to have recorded the feat for their own franchise. Giannis was no longer just potential, he was joining the greats like Dave Cowens, Scottie Pippen, Kevin Garnett, and Lebron James as a franchise player who could dominate the stat boards for his team.

Giannis was named All-NBA Second Team that season as well as becoming the first Bucks player ever to win the NBA Most Improved Player award. He led his team to the playoffs where they faced off against the Toronto Raptors. Giannis led the charge with three games of 25 or more points, but it wasn't enough as they fell to the Raptors 4–2 in the series. However, it was a huge, momentous year for Giannis. Not only had he begun to fill out physically, but his game was also reaching heights that nobody could have ever imagined he would achieve. This phenomenal performance helped the Bucks franchise in extending Giannis's contract and increasing it to $100 million dollars.

Transforming Into a Superstar

Although not all players have a great season and then can come back and perform at the same level the following year. Giannis was able to continue many of the things that he'd started the year before when the 2017-2018 season rolled around. In fact, after just the first week, Giannis was named the Eastern Conference Player of the Week, and many were excited to see him lead the Bucks to a great season. He didn't disappoint.

In the first four games, he started the season off with 30 or more points in each game. His 147 points from those four games were the most over the first four games in a season by anyone in NBA history. He even beat out Kareem Abdul-Jabber, the former record holder, who had 146 in the first four games of the 1970-1971 season. Additionally, he kept his excellent performance going with twenty or more points and at least five rebounds in 27 consecutive games, the longest streak since Shaquille O'Neal in the 2000-2001 season.

Later that season, he even managed his ninth triple-double when the Bucks faced the Denver Nuggets, making Giannis the Buck with the most triple-doubles. He took that one away from Kareem as well. However, his great play was not enough to keep the Bucks going for long in the postseason as they fell to the Boston Celtics in the first round, defeated in game seven.

The following year in 2018, Giannis continued to help lead his team by putting up great numbers and making plays that opened things up for his teammates. The Bucks began the season 4–0, for the first time since the 2001-2002 season, thanks, in part, to the excellent performance that Giannis gave against the Philadelphia 76ers. Leading his team with 32 points and 18 rebounds as well as 10 assists, Giannis didn't just secure the triple-double, but also the 123–108 win over the Sixers, too. That game marked the fourth game in a row that Giannis had over 25 points and 15 rebounds. Since that was four consecutive games as the season openers, Giannis was the first player since Wilt Chamberlain, a fantastic 54 years before, to accomplish the feat.

Continuing on throughout the season, Giannis would have stints of games where he would be on fire, bringing in 25 or more points per game for weeks at a time. When they faced the Cleveland Cavaliers that December, Giannis scored 44 points, matching his career-high as they won 114-102. Later that month, he pulled in his third triple-double of the season against the Nets.

His performance was again earning him recognition from across the league, and he received the Eastern Conference Player of the Month for three months in a row from October to December. He was the first player in Bucks franchise history to win the award back-to-back multiple times. And this wasn't even into the heart of the season yet.

As if he hadn't already set and broken enough records in the first half of the season and in previous ones. Giannis continued to shine and show the world that he was no longer the kid who couldn't make a layup. He was no longer the young man who many thought should be sent down to the developmental league. He wasn't the skinny rookie that was just hoping to keep his head afloat any longer. Instead, Giannis was carving out a piece of the NBA out for himself and solidifying his name in its history.

Later that season, he went on to break Shaquille O'Neal's record for the most games in a single season to put up more than 25 points, 15 rebounds, and five assists. He broke his career-high 44 points by scoring 52 points and 16 rebounds when they faced off against the 76ers again. When the two teams would meet once more, Giannis pulled down another 13 rebounds and 45 points, helping the Bucks to clinch the number one spot in the Eastern Conference.

For the first time in almost twenty years, the Bucks made it past the first round of playoffs, where they swept the Detroit Pistons in four games. When he scored 41 points in that fourth game, Giannis again put his name in the record books alongside some of the greatest players in Bucks and NBA history. He was just the fifth player in franchise history to score more than forty in a game in a playoff series. He joined the ranks with Kareem Abdul-Jabber, Terry Cummings, Ray Allen, and Michael Redd. They even made it to the Eastern Conference Finals before being defeated by the Toronto Raptors, who came back and won four straight games after being down to the Bucks 2–0.

That season, people were really beginning to see Giannis as the face of the franchise. He had not only proven that he could perform, but he was doing it so well that it traversed seasons. He has proven himself as one of the greatest players that the Bucks had ever had. He was also drawing attention and became someone that everyone in the league was talking about. At the end of the season, he was even awarded the NBA's Most Valuable Player, making him only the second Milwaukee player besides Abdul-Jabber to win the award. He was also the third-youngest player to win it, coming in behind Derrick Rose and LeBron James. As a Greek citizen, he was also only the fifth person born outside of the US to win the award.

When looking back at the draft analysis and the potential that Giannis had in coming to the league, nobody, absolutely nobody, could have guessed that they were looking at a future All-Star and MVP. While he had talent and the build that would later fill out, it wasn't until he really got going in the league that he began to come into his own.

Undoubtedly, it is thanks to the Milwaukee coaches and staff that Giannis has become the player that he is today. Not only did they have the vision to pick him up in the draft, but they provided him with the trainers and coaches that he needed not just to bulk up but to level up his game as well. Additionally, Milwaukee has provided a home for Giannis and his family. If it weren't for his ability to play in the NBA, there is no telling where Giannis or his family would have ended up. Still, thankfully, nobody will ever know because he is continuing to rock the arena every time he steps foot on the court.

Representative Teams

Although Giannis was doing well in the NBA, he never stopped looking at his basketball career from an international standpoint. Even though he hadn't gone on to play for the Spanish team that he'd first signed with, Giannis made it a point to represent his home country of Greece when he could.

The first time he represented Greece was back before he went into the draft during 2013 in the FIBA Under 20 Championship. His performance there had not only served to make Greece proud, but it helped to launch him into the NBA by giving the scouts there a first-hand view of what he could do for their teams.

Additionally, he played for the Senior team in 2014 at the FIBA Basketball World Cup. They finished ninth that year and Giannis averaged 6.3 points and 4.3 rebounds. Still, it was an excellent experience for him after joining the NBA and being able to travel and play how he wanted to play.

The following year, he continued to play for Greece in the EuroBasket 2015. Their team was undefeated in pool play, sending them to face off against Spain. However, the Greeks weren't enough to defeat the Spanish side, who ended up winning the whole tournament. Giannis performed well, with three double-doubles that tournament.

Playing for Greece was bittersweet. Although many in the country would have shunned him when he was younger and denied him citizenship despite being born there, Giannis still felt the patriotism and loyalty to Greece, having absorbed the culture after living there his entire life. Being able to represent Greece on multiple occasions helped solidify not only Giannis but the value of those who were immigrants in Greece as well. He became a role model and a face of success to the thousands of those who were still being persecuted and put down because they weren't seen as citizens.

PERSONAL LIFE

After his rookie year, Giannis was able to provide enough money for his family to be able to move to the United States and be with him. Not everyone came, however, since all of the boys seemed to have different athletic-based paths in front of them.

Thanasis, who had come with Giannis and had been drafted to the developmental league, was later drafted by the New York Knicks in 2014. However, after a short time there, he moved back to Greece, where he still plays today for the Panathinaikos.

His older brother, Francis, who had originally stayed in Nigeria with their grandparents, eventually went on to follow in their father's footsteps, playing professional soccer in Nigeria. However, he later moved to Greece, where he played both soccer and basketball.

Their younger brother, Kostas, who played for the Filathlitikos the year after Thanasis and Giannis moved to the US, went on to play basketball in college. He attended Dayton and then was later drafted to the NBA by the Dallas Mavericks, joining his brother in the league in 2018.

In the summer of 2016, both Giannis and Thanasis were called back home to Greece to fulfill some of their Greek duties. For all Greek citizens who permanently live overseas, they are required to do three months of service in the Greek military. That summer, the brothers made their way home to train and fulfill their obligation to their home country. Even though the expectation is three months, because they are professional athletes, leeway was given to them. This helped ensure that they did not end up missing any pre-season workouts with their teams. After serving their time at the training, they headed back to the US, happy to have served the country that they represent.

When Giannis can, he still visits his home country for his own purposes as well. He makes it a point to go back and visit some of the people there that helped him to get where he is today. In fact, one of the people that he makes sure to visit is Giannis Tsiggas, the café owner that used to give Giannis and his younger brothers food. Tsiggas did this for the boys for free, knowing that their whole family was working hard, and they were continually struggling to have enough to go around.

Tsiggas did this despite the backlash that he got from other Greeks who didn't look fondly upon anyone who did favors for non-Greek immigrants or their families. Still, Giannis remembers him fondly and makes sure that the world knows just how much Tsiggas means to him. Hanging in his shop are two items that Giannis brought after returning from America. The first is a photo frame that contains two pictures. The first photo is of Giannis and Tsiggas when Giannis was just a boy. The second photo is them together recently, showing the growth Giannis had and how far he had come. The second item that Tsiggas has hanging in his shop is Giannis's All-Star jersey, which is framed behind the counter as a gift that Giannis gave to his old friend.

Traveling through that old neighborhood, it is also clear that they value Giannis and his story, showcasing that he was from there with a commemorative mural. The mural just so happens to be painted on the basketball court that was the very court that Giannis and Thanasis played on when they were only seven or eight years old. It is the same court where he and Giannis would have to switch shoes to play on, both of them bumbling around with a ball. Looking at either of them now, it is clear that they are no longer the same boys, but they will always remember where they came from.

Greece still struggles with issues when it comes to dealing kindly and respectfully towards immigrants. But there are many there, both citizens and non-citizens alike who are watching Giannis's journey in awe. For the Greeks, although they had initially seen him as an outsider, he is now very much revered as one of their own. For those who immigrated to Greece, or those who are still being put down as "other" they see Giannis as the first of their own to have made it big. Not only that, but many of them also look up to him as a guidepost and shining light for what their lives can become despite how hard it is currently.

Even if situations in Greece and other places around the world are still tenuous and troublesome, Giannis has proven to the world that so many things can challenge a person. Yet, that person can still thrive and excel anyways. Giannis has started a conversation in the world about what it means to be a Greek from African origins. He has unwittingly become a role model on what it means to follow your dreams.

While on the court, his confidence and competitive spirit take the forefront of his persona. Once off of it though, he reverts back to the kind and humble Giannis that so many have come to admire and respect. Once people learn about his history and his background, they can see the reasons why this young man is still able to look at all he has and always be grateful for it. Some, however, might question how it is that he can look back so quickly and remember just the good in times that must have been incredibly hard. However, he does it. It is clear that Giannis is someone whose spirit simply cannot be broken, and basketball fans around the world look forward to watching where his journey may take him next.

MORE FROM JACKSON CARTER BIOGRAPHIES

My goal is to spark the love of reading in young adults around the world. Too often children grow up thinking they hate reading because they are forced to read material they don't care about. To counter this we offer accessible, easy to read biographies about sportspeople that will give young adults the chance to fall in love with reading.

Go to the Website Below to Join Our Community

https://mailchi.mp/7cced1339ff6/jcbcommunity

Or Find Us on Facebook at

www.facebook.com/JacksonCarterBiographies

As a Member of Our Community You Will Receive:

First Notice of Newly Published Titles

Exclusive Discounts and Offers

Influence on the Next Book Topics

Don't miss out, join today and help spread the love of reading around the world!

OTHER WORKS BY JACKSON CARTER BIOGRAPHIES

Made in the USA
Columbia, SC
09 December 2020

27113175R00024